This book belongs to:

Ashley and joey

FURRY WILD ANIMALS AND FRIENDS!

Share-A-Book

Squirrels move quickly through trees and have no fear of high places as they jump from branch to branch. Their long, fluffy tails are used for balance.

The mouse is a very small, quick creature. Mice scurry about hunting for food and they will eat almost anything. Being very bold, they can often be found in unusual places.

Chipmunks are quick and curious animals. They hunt for nuts, berries, grains and seeds to store as food for their hibernation period during the winter months.

Raccoons sleep during the day and scavenge for food at night. They look like bandits with their mask-like markings.

The fox looks very much like a small dog. They spend much of their day resting so they can hunt at night.

Deer live in the forests and swamps of North America. They are known for being very graceful and they can run quickly.

Rabbits are easily recognized by their large ears and fluffy tails. They have strong back legs to help them jump.

The opossum likes to sleep hanging upside down by its tail. It will play dead when it feels threatened by danger.

When skunks feel they are in danger, they will lift their tails and spray a very strong smelling liquid. This odor scares away the skunk's attackers.

Mountain lions can jump up to twenty feet in one leap. They are strong and quick hunters who live mostly in the western United States.

Beavers like to spend their time swimming in cold water. They use their long, sharp teeth to chop down trees and their wide, flat tails to pack down the mud used in building their lodges and dams.

Porcupines are covered with sharp spines called quills. Since they move very slowly, the quills help protect the porcupines from their enemies.

Otters live in dens along riverbanks.
They are very playful and like to swim
and slide in the mud along the riverside.

Brown bears are usually vegetarians, but they will sometimes catch fish or small animals for food.

Timber wolves
live in groups
called "packs."

One wolf leads
the pack and
they rarely fight
with each other.

**Look for other
titles in this series:**

Beautiful Zoo Animals
Friendly Farm Animals
Incredible Dinosaurs